Surrounded
By Beauty

Surrounded By Beauty

PICTURES OF CYPRUS WITH
40 ENCOURAGING BIBLE VERSES

Olive Wilson

ISBN-13: 979-8-8512-3482-8

Dedication

This book is dedicated to my parents, who have stood by me through the years and helped me in many ways during my years at home and abroad.

Thank you to my artist friend, Olja Lazarevska, who inspired me to look at life through a camera lens. Heartfelt thanks also to my niece, Hannah Booth, for editing the book.

Thank you to everyone else who has supported me faithfully and prayerfully over the past years. Thank you for all the advice, letters and emails of encouragement from the many Christians who are wonderful mentors and examples in the faith. You know who you are!

May the scenes of Cyprus inspire you to rejoice in God's creational glory and contemplate the encouraging exhortations of His Word.

Almond blossom

I will never leave thee, nor forsake thee.

Hebrews 13:5

As we look at the beauty of nature in our surroundings, God's majestic touch is evident. It is a constant reminder that He is in control of this world and its events. He has promised to be with His people and will never fail or abandon us. What a comfort, not only for the good times but also for the moments of trial we will inevitably encounter through this journey of life.

Oh love that will not let me go
I rest my weary soul in thee
I give thee back the life I owe
That in thine ocean depths its flow
May richer, fuller be. [1]

Sea Caves, Cape Greco

The LORD is my rock, and my fortress, and my deliverer; my God, my strength, in whom I will trust.

Psalm 18:2

&

Contemplation

The Psalmist David trusted in the One who is immovable and firm as a rock. Governments, world views and values have changed through the ages, but our God never changes. He remains constant and keeps His eternal promises.

We can be sure that what He has ordained concerning future events will surely come to pass at the appointed time. There is no greater assurance in life than to trust in God our Rock.

Great is Thy faithfulness,
O God my Father,
There is no shadow of
turning with Thee.
Thou changest not,
Thy compassions, they fail not,
As Thou hast been,
Thou forever will be. [2]

Limassol Marina

**I will instruct thee and teach thee in
the way which thou shalt go:
I will guide thee with mine eye.**

Psalm 32:8

God promises to be our guide through His inerrant Word, which instructs us in every aspect of life. Even when we wander off the path, He graciously brings us back and prepares the way. We are called to walk faithfully with Him in the direction He has designed for us.

When we are trying to discern the course of our path, there may be a time of waiting before the way becomes clear. The Lord guides those who sincerely desire to do His will *in His time*. While God's general plan is revealed in Scripture, uncovering His specific plan necessitates prayer, patience and faith. The Bible states that God opens and closes doors; a door closing can often signify the opening of a new chapter, which leads us deeper into the Lord's will.

With fear and trembling we must rely upon God for guidance in the inner depths. This is the sole way to walk according to the spirit.

Watchman Nee

Daisy

**I have loved thee with an everlasting love:
therefore with lovingkindness
have I drawn thee.**

Jeremiah 31:3

☙

While this verse was originally directed towards God's people Israel in the Old Testament, it is the same God who saves us through the sacrifice of His Son and draws us to Himself. His love is unconditional and unchanging. We often do not feel worthy of His love, but Christ's perfect sacrifice means we can be accepted and loved by God's grace alone.

As God's people, we can trace the hand of God's goodness and steadfast love in our walk with Him. Let us give thanks for God's everlasting love, care, compassion and blessings with hearts of worship and praise!

Loved with everlasting love
Led by grace that love to
know;
Spirit, breathing from above,
Thou hast taught me it is so.
Oh, this full and perfect peace!
Oh, this transport all divine!
In a love which cannot cease,
I am His, and He is mine. [3]

Ayia Napa

And he said unto them, Come ye yourselves apart into a desert place, and rest a while.

Mark 6:31

☙

We live in an increasingly demanding world with busy schedules and challenges. Prolonged periods of stress in difficult work environments can lead to adverse reactions in the body. The Lord recognised the danger of burnout and tells His disciples to rest in the context of Mark 6. They heed His advice and on retreating to a desolate place, are followed by crowds. This generates the 'feeding of the five thousand', after which the Lord departs alone to the mountain to pray. If the Lord needed to retire from the crowds to spend time alone with His Father, how much more do we need to adopt this habit!

A day or two at the seaside may be what the doctor ordered! Science tells us that looking at the sea impacts our brains and mental health. The colour blue has a calming effect and the fresh, salty air relaxes our minds. The feeling of sand under our toes is soothing, reminding us of the happy, carefree days of our childhood.

Refreshed souls are more effective in Christian ministry and the workplace. With increased energy and mental alertness, we can create and work more efficiently. God's presence can be felt more intensely when surrounded by scenes of natural beauty, leading us to commune with Him in peace. He will meet us in the still moments when we seek His face; take time to retreat into His presence for a time of respite and renewal.

Limassol sunset

**Thou wilt keep him in perfect peace,
whose mind is stayed on thee:
because he trusteth in thee.**

Isaiah 26:3

໖ຠ

The word 'shalom' in Hebrew incorporates the idea of peace, well-being, prosperity, fullness, rest, harmony and the absence of agitation or discord. This *perfect peace* (*shalom shalom*) comes solely from an unwavering trust in the Prince of *shalom*. When we keep our minds focused on Him, we will trust Him with our hearts. It is not an occasional coming to the Lord, but a continuous, steadfast fixation of our minds on the Source of peace.

In 1873, after devastatingly losing his four daughters at sea, Horatio Spafford penned the famous hymn which has brought solace to thousands of Christians, 'It Is Well With My Soul'. He experienced that *shalom* peace in the face of colossal tragedy. What a loss, yet he turned to God in his deep grief and received 'peace like a river'. The Lord promises us a peace that the world does not know.

When peace like a river attendeth my way
when sorrow like sea billows roll;
whatever my lot, Thou hast taught me to say,
"It is well, it is well, with my soul". [4]

Village life – Lefkara

Rejoicing in hope; patient in tribulation; continuing instant in prayer.

Romans 12:12

Lefkara

The quiet villages in Cyprus testify to the unhurried, consistent lives of past generations, who were content to spend their days in calm, tranquil settings. Believers have a joyful hope, making us satisfied and patient in tribulation. High levels of anxiety can be caused by our daily challenges, therefore we need to look beyond ourselves for sustenance and succour with quiet perseverance.

Our strength comes from a prayerful dependence on the Living God, whom we are to trust in all circumstances, with the assurance that He will bless us with His enduring presence. We often forget that such sustaining power is available!

Simply trusting every day,
Trusting through a stormy way;
Even when my faith is small,
Trusting Jesus, that is all. [5]

Paphos Lighthouse

**Thy word is a lamp unto my feet,
and a light unto my path.**

Psalm 119:105

A lighthouse is an inspiring symbol of hope, safety and security. Without it, many ships would run aground on the rocky seabed and founder. The guiding light ensures the ship's path is illuminated by powerful flashes, enabling it to find its way safely to the harbour.

Similarly, the Bible is God's guiding light for our life on earth. It should not be regarded solely as a rule book; it is a revelation of God's heart and plan to redeem the world, with instructions of wisdom to protect us. Light and hope emanate from His Word in a dark, chaotic world. Reading the inspired, enlightening words illuminates our walk by revealing what God's standard requires.

For the word of God is quick, and powerful, and sharper than any two-edged sword, piercing even to the dividing asunder of soul and spirit, and of the joints and marrow, and is a discerner of the thoughts and intents of the heart. Hebrews 4:12

Kolossi Castle

The LORD is good, a strong hold in the day of trouble; and he knoweth them that trust in him.

Nahum 1:7

℘

Kyrenia Castle

Castles and fortresses remind us of a day when a stronghold was needed against a literal enemy. As many Christians come under attack in the spiritual realm and face adversity, we can resort to Almighty God. He knows His own and provides refuge and protection in the face of the enemy's schemes.

We are exhorted to put on our spiritual armour; *the breastplate of righteousness, the gospel of peace* on our feet, *the shield of faith, the helmet of salvation* and *the sword of the Spirit* (Ephesians 6). Only then can we withstand Satan's attacks with the resources God has given to each believer.

A mighty fortress is our God,
a bulwark never failing;
our helper he, amid the flood
of mortal ills prevailing.
For still our ancient foe
does seek to work us woe;
his craft and power are great,
and armed with cruel hate,
on earth is not his equal. [6]

Larnaca Salt Lake

... whatsoever things are true, whatsoever things are honest, whatsoever things are just, whatsoever things are pure, whatsoever things are lovely, whatsoever things are of good report; if there be any virtue, and if there be any praise, think on these things.

Philippians 4:8

&

Greater Flamingos

Flamingos are grey when they are born. They turn pink from the high levels of beta-carotene in their diet of brine shrimps, crustaceans and blue-green algae. Their unique bills are used upside-down to filter feed, separating mud and silt from their food intake.

This reflects a spiritual truth: *we are what we eat!* Just as the depth of colour in the flamingos reflects the levels of beta-carotene consumed, the depth of our Christian walk will manifest how much we have been feeding on the Word of God. The more we digest God's Word, the more we will reflect His character.

We also need to 'filter feed', rejecting what is essentially harmful to our spiritual purity. We are exhorted to meditate on what is honest, just, pure and praiseworthy. This will be visible in our conduct as we mature in the Lord.

Damask rose

**And let the beauty of the Lord our God be up-
on us: and establish thou the work
of our hands upon us.**

Psalm 90:17

&

Frangipani (plumeria rubra)

God's beauty will be reflected in our lives if we permit Him to lead us fully according to His purposes of love. By staying close to Him, the fragrance of His presence will go with us. Just as the sweet nectar attracts bees to the flowers, a sweet, kind demeanour becomes an attractive trait in our Christian character.

Others will marvel when we act in a Christ-like manner under pressure and will be drawn to knowing the Saviour through our personal testimony. The book of Proverbs has much to say, for example, about controlling our tongues: *A soft answer turns away wrath, but a harsh word stirs up anger* (Proverbs 15:1 ESV).

Beautiful Saviour!
Lord of all the nations!
Son of God and Son of Man!
Glory and honour,
praise, adoration,
now and forevermore be thine. [7]

1500 – year old Olive Tree

But the fruit of the Spirit is love, joy, peace, longsuffering, gentleness, goodness, faith, meekness, temperance: against such there is no law.

Galatians 5:22-23

Cyprus yields a rich array of fruit and agricultural produce throughout the year due to the Mediterranean climate. Orange trees release a fresh fragrance into the air, along with splendid lemon trees in numerous gardens throughout the island.

As we give more of ourselves over to the control of the indwelling Holy Spirit and spend time in the sunshine of the Lord's presence, His fruit will appear in our lives. We are to be known as Christians by the manifestation *of love, joy, peace, longsuffering, gentleness, goodness, faith, meekness* and *temperance. Fruit of the Spirit* is in the singular, meaning that all components will be present.

Fruit is always the miraculous, the created; it is never the result of willing, but always a growth. The fruit of the Spirit is a gift of God, and only He can produce it. They who bear it know as little about it as the tree knows of its fruit. They know only the power of Him on whom their life depends.

Dietrich Bonhoeffer

Limassol Old Port at sunset

Casting all your care upon him; for he careth for you.

1 Peter 5:7

ℰℭ

Just as fishermen cast their nets into the sea from their fishing boats, so are we to cast our cares on the Lord. Often we become encumbered with huge burdens which are too heavy to carry. The Lord Jesus cares for us with indescribable love and invites us to entrust Him with our daily woes and distress. When we have ensured that the source of the problem is not our own behaviour, we are to commit it to the Lord and leave it there.

Once we have asked Him to take our *load of care*, we can be free from that all-consuming apprehension that often besets us. Our peace of mind depends on how much we trust Him to intervene directly and effect change in our circumstances. God's peace, which *passes all understanding, shall keep your hearts and minds through Christ Jesus* (Philippians 4:7). His peace promotes health and prosperity of the soul; we can always return to Him regardless of how far we have walked on the path of self-reliance, surrendering our souls into His loving care.

Are we weak and heavy laden,
cumbered with a load of care?
Precious Saviour, still our refuge-
take it to the Lord in prayer!
Do your friends despise,
forsake you?
Take it to the Lord in prayer!
In his arms he'll take and shield you;
you will find a solace there. [8]

Village door, Fasoula

**Behold, I stand at the door, and knock:
if any man hear my voice, and open the door,
I will come in to him, and will sup with him,
and he with me.**

Revelation 3:20

જી

God the Father of all creation longs to have intimate fellowship with us. Sharing a meal with someone has long been a symbol of friendship; the Lord promises this level of communion to those who hear His voice and accept His presence.

He tenderly invites us to take time out of our packed schedules each day to dine at His table. He also asks those who have never opened their hearts to Him to accept His invitation by faith and invite Him into their lives as Lord and Saviour.

I sat down in the morning
to meet my Lord.
In the hushed stillness around me,
I felt His holy presence
and bowed my head.
I did not speak audibly,
nor did He,
but His whispers
echoed in my heart
and calmed my fears.

Natural beauty

For our light affliction, which is but for a moment, worketh for us a far more exceeding and eternal weight of glory.

2 Corinthians 4:17

Pinks and violets

The Bible speaks of a future glory which will be ours in eternity after the trials and tribulations of this life. Any discouragements of today will be eclipsed by a *far more exceeding and eternal weight of glory!* Suffering is not something we accept gladly, but with the Lord's help and comfort, we can overcome, knowing that it is only for a short while.

Elisabeth Elliot wrote: *If all struggles and sufferings were eliminated, the spirit would no more reach maturity than would the child.* We often do not understand God's permissive will, but we know that all things 'work together for good' to deepen our knowledge of Him and His ways.

When we all get to heaven,
what a day of rejoicing that will be!
When we all see Jesus,
we'll sing and shout the victory! [9]

Crown daisies at the coast

**Bless the LORD, O my soul and all that is within me, bless his holy name....
who crowneth thee with lovingkindness and tender mercies.**

Psalm 103: 1, 4b

&

Coastal scene

Crown daisies decorate much of the coast in spring. Glittering like jewels, their luminous yellow petals reflect the sun's rays. Believers have been crowned with God's lovingkindness and tender mercies as a sign we are His. His light shines through us to bring revelation to others.

Prayer

May those who see me
know I'm Yours,
by the smile of love on my face,
by the kindness on my lips
and the gentleness
of my ways.
May I wear my crown
for all to see,
that they may also desire
to be crowned
with the love and
compassion of my King.

Spring flower

**Blessed be the God and Father of
our Lord Jesus Christ, which according to
his abundant mercy hath begotten us again
unto a lively hope by the resurrection of Jesus Christ from the dead.**

1 Peter 1:3

&

Amathounta, Limassol

The colours and design of God's creation delight our hearts particularly in spring, the time of year which reminds us of resurrection to life. Flowers and foliage emerge vibrantly after the sleep of winter and the animal kingdom welcomes the brighter days with rejuvenation.

After the sleep of death, those who are *in Christ* will rise to everlasting life and our bodies will be changed from corruptible to incorruptible (1 Corinthians 15:53). Our lowly bodies will be conformed to Christ's glorious body (Philippians 3:21). This is the sure hope and joy of every believer!

*On that bright and
cloudless morning when
the dead in Christ shall rise,
And the glory of his
resurrection share;
When his chosen ones
shall gather to their
home beyond the skies,
And the roll is called up
yonder I'll be there.* [10]

St George's Harbour

Let us therefore come boldly unto the throne of grace, that we may obtain mercy, and find grace to help in time of need.

Hebrews 4:16

Fishing boats at St. George's Harbour

When facing life's challenges, we are often tempted to turn to various sources for assistance. While mature Christians can offer advice from their years of experience, we are exhorted to seek divine sustenance and guidance.

Our Great High Priest, who experienced human life as a Man, invites us to come *boldly* to heaven's throne. He does not expect us to accomplish tasks through our own efforts. The New Testament records that the veil of the temple was torn in two at the time of the Lord's crucifixion, opening the way into God's holy presence for all to come through faith.

Help is readily available from the *throne of grace* through the Lord's mercy. He knows our every need and understands our shortcomings because He too *was in all points tempted as we are, yet without sin.* Hebrews 4:15. The Holy Spirit aids us in our weakness by interceding for us with *groanings which cannot be uttered.*

Agios Georgios Alamanou Beach

Let every thing that hath breath praise the Lord. Praise ye the Lord.

Psalm 150:6

જી

Beach art

The Bible tells us that all creation was made for God's glory (Colossians 1:16) and that we are to offer continually a *sacrifice of praise* (Hebrews 13:15). The Lord expressed on one occasion that the rocks would cry out if people did not worship Him. We read in Revelation of the four living creatures around the throne who incessantly cry out in worship day and night: *Holy, holy, holy, Lord God Almighty, which was, and is, and is to come* (Revelation 4:8).

We praise Him not only for His majesty in creation but also for His eternal salvation. If we have accepted the surpassing love of Christ and His saving forgiveness, our redeemed hearts will joyfully express our gratitude in praise and worship!

Beach scene

Follow me, and I will make you fishers of men.

Matthew 4:19

છ

The joy of knowing the Gospel and having our sins forgiven should make us desire to reach out to others with this message of God's grace. The Lord called His disciples to be *fishers of men*, devoting their time to winning souls. They at once obeyed His call, leaving behind what they deemed precious to follow their Master into the unknown. They would have to rely solely on God's provision after forsaking their professions to be part of the Lord's chosen group of disciples.

As God leads, we are to cast our nets in deep waters and look to Him for the spiritual 'catch'. All around there are broken lives who do not know where to find hope and fortitude for living. How will they hear if we do not freely proclaim the marvellous, liberating truth of the Gospel?  There are many forms of media we can now use to spread God's Word in ways that will speak to searching hearts. Take time to meet others right where they are today and share the good news of the Gospel.

Lace umbrellas, Nicosia

**For we are his workmanship,
created in Christ Jesus unto good works,
which God hath before ordained that
we should walk in them.**

Ephesians 2:10

In the Cypriot village of Lefkara, ladies sit outdoors and skilfully produce embroidery known as *lefkaritiko* and other attractive handicrafts, a village practice dating back to the 15th century. Silver goods are also crafted by hand in several workshops in the village. In our fast-paced world, this is a dying trade which is being carefully preserved by a handful of dedicated locals.

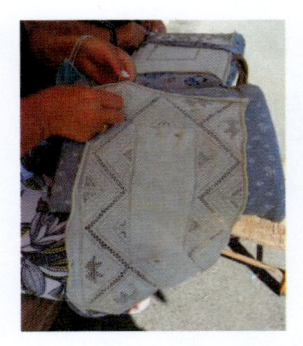

The Bible tells us that we are God's 'workmanship', created for good works which God has prepared beforehand in our walk with Him. The word 'workmanship' is *poiema* in Greek, the word from which our word 'poem' is derived. We are His unique 'poems', compositions which give expression to our Creator's design and purpose for humanity. We are to know God through His Son and perform His will on the earth for His glory. This is the true calling of every believer and can only be fulfilled by walking in the Spirit through Christ. The Westminster Shorter Catechism sums up our purpose on earth: *Man's chief end is to glorify God and to enjoy Him forever.*

Sunrise in Limassol

**From the rising of the sun unto
the going down of the same the LORD's
name is to be praised.**

Psalm 113:3

&

For many of us, the morning is a time of tranquillity and stillness when we can commune with God. However, the verse from Psalm 113 gives a whole day's scope to praise His name. Whether morning or evening, it is desirable to have a 'quiet time' when we can read the Bible and worship the Lord.

Thankful hearts are happy hearts and time spent with the Lord gives us spiritual strength to face the day. Throughout the day there are many opportunities to offer a silent prayer to the Lord. The Bible tells us to pray without ceasing, which means we can have a prayerful spirit as we go about our daily business.

Take time to be holy,
speak oft with thy Lord;
Abide in Him always,
and feed on His Word.
Make friends of God's children,
help those who are weak,
Forgetting in nothing
His blessing to seek. [11]

Larnaca

**Ask, and it shall be given you; seek,
and ye shall find; knock, and it shall
be opened unto you.**

Matthew 7:7

⦵

The Lord invites us to ask from a generous God who loves to give. Just as a good father heeds the requests of his children, our heavenly Father lends an ear to our prayers. However, we need to judge if we are asking amiss because the One who knows the end from the beginning sometimes withholds granting our desires for our own good. We are also reminded in the New Testament that we do not receive because we do not ask. We are to ask with spiritual wisdom and discernment in the name of Jesus, according to His will.

I thank you, Lord, You were too wise to heed
My feeble prayers, and answer as I sought,
Since these rich gifts Your bounty has bestowed
Have brought me more than all I asked or thought;
Giver of good, so answer each request
With Your own giving, better than my best.

Annie Johnston Flint.

Sunflowers

... one thing I do, forgetting those things which are behind, and reaching forth unto those things which are before, I press toward the mark for the prize of the high calling of God in Christ Jesus.

Philippians 3:13-14

സ

When we take a backward look at our lives, we wish we had the wisdom in earlier years that we currently possess. The university of life is a learning curve we must experience, inevitably marked with failures and mistakes. If we continuously look back, however, our forward path will be hindered by regrets and nostalgia. Our minds will be beset with doubt and fear, which is the opposite of God's desire for us. The apostle Paul exhorts us to forget the past and to focus on the future so we can accomplish our calling.

Our goal is to aim for the *prize of the high calling* we have in the Lord. Paul is exemplary in striving for excellence in life's race through unwavering commitment. He aptly exhorts the Corinthian believers to run the race with self-control and discipline to receive the incorruptible prize of knowing Christ and being with Him for all eternity. The years given to us on earth is our time and opportunity of service. Let us go forward with renewed vision to serve the Lord, adopting undivided hearts and steadfast minds.

Salamis, North Cyprus

For whatsoever things were written aforetime were written for our learning, that we through patience and comfort of the scriptures might have hope.

Romans 15:4

&

The Bible, an anthology originally written in Hebrew, Aramaic and Koine Greek, maintains a delightful harmony and continuity within. Written by 40 authors and 'God-breathed', it was composed over a period of 1400 years. What a privilege to hold this precious book in our hands in our mother tongue thousands of years after the first words were written. We are indebted to the Jewish Masoretes and to the church patriarchs, who meticulously copied and preserved Biblical manuscripts for centuries. We also are not unmindful of the skilled translators and publishers who have laboured tirelessly throughout history, some of whom were burned at the stake. The Bible, God's living Word, is not only unique but also a priceless treasure.

It is reassuring to recognise the fulfilled prophecies regarding the Lord's coming to the earth and His death - more than four hundred prophecies have been fulfilled precisely by *Yeshua* (Jesus). Eschatological truths also inspire believers to maintain hope, even if the world appears to be spiralling out of control. Our Sovereign God is still on the throne!

Spring flowers

**Let all the earth fear the LORD;
Let all the inhabitants of the world
stand in awe of Him.**

Psalm 33:8

☙

Children often walk around with wide eyes as they encounter new experiences. With maturity, we tend to lose this sense of awe. We form habits and lose our sense of adventure and delight. As believers, we can become so familiar with Bible passages and Christian truth that we sometimes gloss over them. Reading a different translation of a passage can impact its meaning dynamically and refresh its application.

A sense of awe can be retained by looking at nature and seeing God's majestic power in creation. When we remember how great He is and how dependent we are on His lovingkindness and grace, we are led to worship. Alistair Begg sums it up befittingly: 'Only when we are captured by an overwhelming sense of awe and reverence in the presence of God, will we begin to worship God in spirit and in truth.'

Winter sea, Limassol

The LORD is my shepherd;
I shall not want.

Psalm 23:1

&

It goes without saying that every day is not filled with cloudless sunshine, even in Cyprus; this is also the case in our lives, figuratively speaking. Occasionally the waves billow and the winds blow, bringing need and instability into our path. In those times, we can look to the Shepherd who promises we will never be in want. John's Gospel reminds us that the Lord is the 'Good Shepherd' who *lays down His life for the sheep* (John 10:11). We know His voice and like the sheep, come to the One who cares for us and leads us to safety.

The Lord IS my shepherd. Not was, not may be, nor will be. . . is my shepherd on Sunday, is on Monday, and is through every day of the week; is in January, is in December, and every month of the year, is at home, and is in China; is in peace, and is in war; in abundance, and in penury.

Hudson Taylor

Limassol Promenade

**For God so loved the world, that he gave
his only begotten Son, that whosoever be-
lieveth in him should not perish,
but have everlasting life.**

John 3:16

&

The message of God's love is central throughout the Bible. When American ex-footballer, Tim Tebow, was playing in the National Championship in 2009, he wrote the reference John 3:16 on his eye black. He was told two days later that during the match, 94 million people had googled the reference and would consequently have read that precious verse. This is the essence of the Christian message which we need to share with everyone on this planet. There is no other message as vital to each individual as the one contained in John 3:16.

Could we with ink the ocean fill,
And were the skies of parchment made;
Were every stalk on earth a quill,
And every man a scribe by trade;
To write the love of God above
Would drain the ocean dry;
Nor could the scroll contain the whole,
Though stretched from sky to sky. [12]

Daisy

And walk in love, as Christ also hath loved us, and hath given himself for us an offering and a sacrifice to God for a sweet-smelling savour.

Ephesians 5:2

&

Common Lantana

As Christians, we are commanded to walk in love, just as Christ loved us sacrificially and gave His life for us. We bear His name and are called to love as He did through the Holy Spirit, who has poured out His love into our hearts. He taught that this would be a sign we are His followers if we love one another.

The first Christians were renowned for their sacrificial care towards their fellow believers in the hostile Roman world. Luke records in Acts: *And all who believed were together and had all things in common. And they were selling their possessions and belongings and distributing the proceeds to all, as any had need* (Acts 2:44-45 ESV).

But it is mainly the deeds of a love so noble that lead many to put a brand upon us. See, they say, how they love one another...

Tertullian

Coastal cat

**And whatsoever ye do in word or deed,
do all in the name of the Lord Jesus, giving
thanks to God and the Father by him.**

Colossians 3:17

℘

All that we say and do should be to the glory of the Lord, with thanksgiving in His name. Grateful people are much healthier, sleep better, have better friendships and think about others more than those who are less appreciative. They do not grumble and complain but look for the good in every situation. A thankful disposition maintains a positive outlook and influence. As we consider our lives, we have much for which we can express appreciation!

Each new day is an opportunity to render thanks to the God who faithfully sustains us and blesses us abundantly through His grace and mercy. We can be thankful for our salvation, health, homes, families, employment, holidays and stable environment. We can cherish the small pleasures of life, such as a kind word, a smile of appreciation or a delicate flower in the wind. Take time to tell someone why you are grateful for them and show them an unexpected kindness as an expression of heartfelt indebtedness.

Troödos Mountains

Pleasant words are as an honeycomb, sweet to the soul, and health to the bones.

Proverbs 16:24

Pleasant or gracious words are compared to the sweetness of honeycomb in the book of Proverbs. There is much goodness in honeycomb, a substance used medicinally in ancient times. We should never underestimate the effect of our words, especially on children who are tender and impressionable in their formative years.

Our greatest example was the Lord, One who spoke graciously with lips of learning. People marvelled at His gracious words. There are times when His words were sharp through righteous anger, but Proverbs 16:24 applies generally to our speech. Hearts can be healed through tender words and we should guard our tongues to ensure we speak kindly.

Let your speech be always with grace, seasoned with salt, that ye may know how ye ought to answer every man.

Colossians 4:6

Paphos coast

Whereas ye know not what shall be on the morrow. For what is your life? It is even a vapour, that appeareth for a little time, and then vanisheth away.

James 4:14

&

The brevity of life becomes more apparent as we age. Endless summers roll into spent decades that have passed by at an alarming rate. This precious commodity of life is compared to a vapour by James, appearing for a little while and vanishing quickly. The number of our days is determined by God, who grants an average lifespan of seventy to eighty years as recorded in Psalm 90:10. Sadly many do not fulfil this period, leaving us all too soon. It is imperative to be ready!

What are we to do then with the days at our disposal? We are to use them discerningly and pray like the Psalmist: *So teach us to number our days, that we may apply our hearts unto wisdom* (Psalm 90:12). Let us give our best years to the Lord when we are full of vitality and vigour. The

yoke is to be borne in our youth (Lamentations 3:27).

He is no fool who gives what he cannot keep to gain what he cannot lose. Jim Elliot

Bougainvillea at Zygi

That their hearts might be comforted, being knit together in love, and unto all riches of the full assurance of understanding, to the acknowledgement of the mystery of God, and of the Father, and of Christ; in whom are hid all the treasures of wisdom and knowledge.

Colossians 2:2-3

೫

Vibrant bougainvillaea bracts are conspicuous in gardens and villages throughout the island of Cyprus in splendid shades of magenta, pink, orange, yellow and white. A closer look reveals small, delicate white flowers in the centre of the bracts, like a hidden treasure.

Our relationship with Christ provides all the wisdom and knowledge we need for our lives. These hidden treasures are found in Him alone and are uncovered to those who seek them in sincerity and truth. As we grow and discover more of the mystery of God, that which is hidden will be increasingly revealed.

Having the eyes of your hearts enlightened, that you may know what is the hope to which he has called you, what are the riches of his glorious inheritance in the saints.

Ephesians 1:18 (ESV)

Cactus

O God, thou art my God; early will I seek thee: my soul thirsteth for thee, my flesh longeth for thee in a dry and thirsty land, where no water is.

Psalm 63:1

౪

The cactus plant can survive without water for days due to its capacity to store water when it has access to a supply. Its fruit, known as prickly or cactus pairs, is surprisingly juicy and nutritious. However, much care is advised when eating as they truly fit their 'prickly' description! Despite the dangers, many a desert wanderer has been timely refreshed by this treasure in a 'dry and thirsty land', often critically boosting low hydration levels.

The Psalmist David had experience of hot, dry desert conditions in the land of Israel and compares his thirst for water to his thirst for God. How deep was his desire to be in God's presence early in the morning! He also likens his thirst to a deer panting for water in Psalm 42 v 1-2: *As the hart panteth after the water brooks, so panteth my soul after thee, O God. My soul thirsteth for God, for the living God: when shall I come and appear before God?*

What do we thirst after in life? Are we thirsty for God's presence or do we fill our days with passing pleasures and pursuits? Let us not be conformed to the world's momentary attractions but thirst instead for spiritual values, which will last for eternity.

Limassol Old Town

Being confident of this very thing, that he which hath begun a good work in you will perform it until the day of Jesus Christ.

Philippians 1:6

❧

Regardless of how long we have been on the Christian path, we are all still a 'work in progress'. It is comforting to have the assurance that our past sins have been cast into the sea of God's 'forgetfulness' (Micah 7:19). This does not give us a licence to sin and then seek forgiveness continually, a concept called 'cheap grace' by German theologian Dietrich Bonhoeffer. Instead, we are to strive for perfection with God's leading.

The renowned Renaissance sculptor, Michelangelo, summed up the potential of every stone in his hands: *Every block of stone has a statue inside it.* Applied to the new believer, God sees the capacity in each one of us to become *a new creation*. The Bible tells us we have been predestined *to be conformed to the image of his Son* (Romans 8:29); with the empowerment of the Holy Spirit, we are to lay aside the 'old self' and put on the 'new self', being renewed in the spirit of our minds (Ephesians 4:22-24).

A beauty

The Lord thy God in the midst of thee is mighty; he will save, he will rejoice over thee with joy; he will rest in his love, he will joy over thee with singing.

Zephaniah 3:17

God takes pleasure in saving the lost and restoring broken lives and hearts. Only He can save us from the power of sin through His Son and when individuals repent, there is rejoicing in Heaven (Luke 15:10). The Lord is building His Church on earth for a future time of exultation when He will receive us to Himself with the anticipated joy mentioned in Hebrews 12:2.

The Church is portrayed in the Bible as Christ's bride. The bride, fully satisfied with His love, becomes still in His presence with inner calm and assurance. Which bridegroom does not rejoice over his beautifully adorned bride? Our heavenly Bridegroom rejoices over us with singing in the jubilant expectancy of welcoming His bride on a future day.

Let us be glad and rejoice, and give honour to him: for the marriage of the Lamb is come, and his wife hath made herself ready. Revelation 19:7

EDRO III shipwreck, Paphos

**Yet the Lord will command his lovingkindness
in the day time, and in the night his song
shall be with me, and my prayer
unto the God of my life.**

Psalm 42:8

છે

In the dark moments, we sometimes ask God "why?". Why the difficulties? Why the loss of loved ones? Why God, why? We are promised His lovingkindness in the daytime and His songs in the night to help us address the challenging obstacles in our path. The Psalmist gives us permission to ask *why* with the assurance we are not alone. Only when we look at the other side of life's 'tapestry' do we get the complete picture, spun by the Master.

Life is But a Weaving

My life is but a weaving
Between my God and me.
I cannot choose the colors
He weaveth steadily.
Oft' times He weaveth sorrow;
And I in foolish pride
Forget He sees the upper
And I the underside.
Not 'til the loom is silent
And the shuttles cease to fly
Will God unroll the canvas
And reveal the reason why.
The dark threads are as needful
In the weaver's skillful hand
As the threads of gold and silver
In the pattern He has planned.
He knows, He loves, He cares;
Nothing this truth can dim.
He gives the very best to those
Who leave the choice to Him.

Grant C. Tuller

White Cosmos flower

I will praise thee; for I am fearfully and wonderfully made: marvellous are thy works; and that my soul knoweth right well.

Psalm 139:14

&

When we observe the minute detail of nature, we are amazed at the intricacy of its design. The Creator's stamp is on every leaf and bud. The Bible reminds us in Psalm 139 of the origins of each human being; God designed each of us *in secret* and prepared the days which lie before us.

The complexity of our bodies and minds causes us to marvel as science continues to reveal facts regarding our existence. Not only did God write His name into the sequence of our DNA code, but He also placed eternity in our hearts. The world cannot bring us enduring peace and satisfaction because we know inherently that we have been created for another sphere.

If we find ourselves with a desire that nothing in this world can satisfy, the most probable explanation is that we were made for another world.

C.S. Lewis

Sunset, Limassol

Wherefore seeing we also are compassed about with so great a cloud of witnesses, let us lay aside every weight, and the sin which doth so easily beset us, and let us run with patience the race that is set before us.

Hebrews 12:1

It has been said that life is a marathon, not a sprint. Endurance and commitment are required to fulfil our God-given purpose. All wrongdoing and sin must be removed from our lives so we can 'run' for God's glory and hear that final 'well done' after crossing the finishing line.

Never in history have there been more resources for our upbuilding and instruction. Never have there been so many opportunities to travel and spread the Gospel. Let us not lose sight of our ultimate calling in Christ.

Only one life, a few brief years,
Each with its burdens, hopes,
and fears;
Each with its days I must fulfil,
Living for self or in His will;
Only one life, 'twill soon be past,
Only what's done for Christ will last.

C. T. Studd

Latchi harbour at sunset

**Let us hold fast the profession of
our faith without wavering;
(for he is faithful that promised;)**

Hebrews 10:23

Sunsets remind us of the faithfulness of God. We are called to be constant in our walk and hold on firmly to the hope we profess. One day our faith will give way to sight and we will enter the land which does not need the sun. The light of God's glory and the Lamb will illuminate our eternal home and we will be reunited with those who have gone before us. May we be found faithful until He calls us home. *When the Son of Man comes, will he find faith on earth?* (Luke 18:8). *Maranatha!*

It doesn't matter much what happens to us. The one thing that matters is how we meet what happens. Limitations, frustrations – they can't cast the smallest handful of dust on the glory of God. So let us be of good courage. He is leading us through and on, and as for God, His way is perfect.

Amy Carmichael

References

1. O Love That Wilt Not Let Me Go. George Matheson

2. Great Is Thy Faithfulness. Thomas Chisholm

3. Loved With Everlasting Love. George W. Robinson

4. It Is Well With My Soul. Horatio G. Spafford

5. Trusting Jesus. Edgar Page

6. A Mighty Fortress. Martin Luther

7. Fairest Lord Jesus. (Anonymous)

8. What A Friend We Have In Jesus. Joseph Scriven

9. When We All Get To Heaven. E. E. Hewitt

10. When The Roll Is Called Up Yonder. James Black

11. Take Time to be Holy. William D. Longstaff

12. The Love of God Is Greater Far. Frederick M. Lehman

Surrounded by beauty!

Only fear the LORD, and serve him in truth with all your heart: for consider how great things he hath done for you.

1 Samuel 12:24

The LORD bless you and keep you;
The LORD make His face shine upon you,
And be gracious to you;
The LORD lift up His countenance upon you,
And give you peace.

Numbers 6:24-26

Other Publications

A Heart of Wisdom – a 40-day devotional for life's journey.

Available on Amazon: hardback, paperback and Kindle.

Further reading about Cyprus:
www.goodnewsincyprus.com

Printed by Amazon Italia Logistica S.r.l.
Torrazza Piemonte (TO), Italy

50320834R00051